Viktor Frankl

The Lost Interview

and

The Last Lesson

By

Bill Halamandaris

Viktor Frankl

	Page
Introduction	1
The Lost Interview	19
The Last Lesson	58

©Bill Halamandaris
ISBN: 9798648724730

Introduction

Viktor Frankl was the founder of Logotherapy, the Third Viennese School of Psychotherapy, and the author of 39 books, including *Man's Search for Meaning*, identified by the Library of Congress as one of the ten most influential books in the English language.

After reading *Man's Search for Meaning*, I sent Dr. Frankl a letter expressing my admiration. I told him I had stumbled on his book after an extensive period of soul-searching and that I wished I had found it earlier.

This book had a profound impact on me and I told him so. To my surprise, Dr. Frankl answered my letter with a personal note raising questions that encouraged a response.

We exchanged letters several times after that before I found an opportunity to invite him to come to America to keynote a conference I was helping organize.

I met Viktor at the airport late one afternoon in l985 and peppered him with questions as we drove to town. I continued my questioning over dinner and then reluctantly said goodnight.

The next morning, Viktor gave a stirring and thought provoking speech, receiving a standing ovation from the three thousand people attending the conference. As I went to the dais to escort him to a reception in his honor, he scribbled something on his notes and then handed them to me. When I looked at what he had given me, I found he had autographed the text of his speech and inscribed it with a personal note.

After lunch, I walked him back to his room and thanked him for making the long journey from Vienna for one speech. I said good-bye not knowing when, if ever, I would see him again.

Early the next morning, the phone rang at my home. When I answered, I heard Viktor's voice. He said his return flight did not leave until late in the day and he was wondering if I would mind coming to the hotel to spend some time with him.

We spent the entire day together. Though nothing explicit was said, I could tell he was "working on me." Viktor had clearly thought about the questions I had asked the day he arrived and was trying to extend my thinking. He probed and pushed with the gentle, thoughtful persistence of the good psychiatrist he was.

Afterwards, Viktor periodically sent me the text of something he was working on – a speech or an article – and asked what I thought. The question was always phrased as though he was seeking my opinion, but I came to know it was just one more way of extending our dialogue.

In much the same manner, I came to expect a periodic phone call. The ones I liked best were the ones where he said he was going to be somewhere in the United States and wondering if I could I find time to join him. Needless to say, I always "found time."

It's hard to overstate the influence Viktor Frankl had on the direction of the life. I know there are many others who could say the same.

He was born in Vienna on March 26, 1905, the second of three children born to Elsa and Gabriel Frankl. His parents were government employees. His father, Gabriel, served as Director in the Ministry of Social Service in Vienna.

Frankl showed interest in the medical profession at an early age. At the age of three year he said he wanted to be a doctor. By the time he was in high school, he was already studying psychology and philosophy. Two years before his graduation in I921, he gave a speech called "On the Meaning of Life."

At about the same time, he made contact with his hero, Dr. Sigmund Freud. Frankl wrote Freud a letter and included a copy of one of his own papers in it. To his surprise, Freud asked Frankl's permission to publish the paper.

Decades later when we spoke of this incident, Frankl still sounded surprised. "Can you imagine?" he said.

Frankl attended the University of Vienna to formally study his chosen fields of neurology and psychiatry. While still a student, he began actively putting into practice what he was learning and the theories he was developing.

He noticed a disturbing trend among students in Austrian high schools. When grades were reported at the end of the school term, there was a spike in suicides. Frankl spearheaded an initiative to provide free counseling to students, with an emphasis on helping them at the end of the school term. Incredibly, the first year that program was implemented was also the first time that there were no student suicides in Vienna.

From there Frankl moved on to become head of the Vienna Psychiatric Hospital's female suicide prevention program. From 1933 to 1937, he worked with thousands of women who were in danger of committing suicide.

In 1938, Germany invaded Austria. Under the new Nazi regime Jews were not permitted to treat Aryan patients. So, Frankl joined the staff of The Rothschild Hospital in Vienna, the only place in Vienna where Jewish patients could be treated. While he was working there, Frankl applied for a visa to the United States.

"Anti-Semitism was increasing daily," he explained, "and my family and I could see what was coming. Like many people, we began preparing to get out. At the eleventh hour as the Nazis were closing in, the U.S. Consulate informed me a visa had been granted for me to emigrate to the United States. This was the moment I had anticipated for several years and I rushed down to the consulate with great excitement.

"My enthusiasm fled when I realized the visa was only valid for one. I was confronted by the fact that if I escaped to America, I would have to leave my parents behind."

In despair Viktor left the embassy and walked in a daze to a park nearby. Covering the yellow Star of David he was compelled to wear on his chest, he sat on the park bench in agony wondering what to do.

"On one hand," he said, "was safety, the opportunity to work, and nurture my 'brain child' — logotherapy. On the other hand, there was the responsibility to take care of my parents by staying with them in Vienna and, rather than leaving them, to their fate share with them."

What would his parents do if he left, he thought. What could he do if he stayed? Would it make any difference to them or would all be lost?

"At best, if I stayed with my family, I would have the opportunity to be with them and protect them from being deported but who knew for how long before the Gestapo came for us all," Viktor said. "If I stayed, my work and theories would perish with me."

Viktor said he sat there, meditating and praying, for more than an hour. Finally, he realized he could not resolve the matter and got up to go home. As he left, he thought that if there ever was a time that a man could use a sign from God, this would be such a time. The issue was beyond human resolution.

Almost immediately upon entering the apartment he shared with his family, Frankl noticed a stone, a piece of marble, on the mantle over the fireplace. He called his father and asked him, "What is this and why is it here?"

"Oh, Viktor," his father said with some excitement. "I forgot to tell you. I picked it up this morning on the site where the largest synagogue in Vienna stood before the Nazis tore it down."

"And why did you bring it home?" Viktor asked.

"'Because I noticed that it is part of the two tablets whereon the Ten Commandments are engraved – you remember, above the altar?' my father said. In fact, one could see, on the piece of marble, one single Hebrew letter engraved and gilded. 'Even more,' my father said, 'I can tell to which of the Ten Commandments this letter refers because it serves the abbreviation for only one.'"

"I looked at it and had my answer," Viktor said. "It was the commandment that says, 'Honor thy father and thy mother.' At that moment, my decision was clear. I gave up my visa and stayed in Austria."

Frankl married in 1941. His wife Tilly conceived but was not allowed to give birth. She was forced to have an abortion just before Frankl was arrested in l942. His wife and parents were arrested at the same time.

The family was sent to Theresienstadt, a camp in Czechoslovakia. Frankl, his wife, and his mother survived Theresienstadt, but his father did not. He died after only six months in the camp.

In 1944, Frankl was ordered to Auschwitz. His mother was also ordered to go, but Tilly was not. Nevertheless, she chose to share her husband's fate and volunteered to be moved to Auschwitz. After arriving at Auschwitz, Tilly was pushed onward to Bergen-Belsen where she died. She was only 24.

A passage in Man's Search for Meaning describes the depth of their affection.

> "And as we stumbled on for miles, slipping icy spots, supporting each other time and again, dragging one another up and onward, nothing was said, but we both knew: each of us was thinking of his wife. Occasionally I looked at the sky, where the stars were fading and the pink light of the morning was beginning to spread behind a dark bank of clouds.

"But my mind clung to my wife's image, imagining it with an uncanny acuteness. I heard her answering me, saw her smile, her frank and encouraging look. Real or not, her look was then more luminous than the sun, which was beginning to rise. A thought transfixed me: for the first time in my life I saw the truth as it is set into song by so many poets, proclaimed as the final wisdom by so many thinkers. The truth — that love is the ultimate and the highest goal to which man can aspire.

"Then I grasped the meaning of the greatest secret that human poetry and human thought and belief have to impart: *The salvation of man is through love and in love.* I understood how a man who has nothing left in this world still may know bliss, be it only for a brief moment, in the contemplation of his beloved. In a position of utter desolation, when a man cannot express himself in positive action, when his only achievement may consist in enduring his sufferings in the right way — an honorable way — in such a position man can, through loving contemplation of the image he carries of his beloved, achieve fulfillment. For the first time in my life I was able to understand the meaning of the words, 'The angels are lost in perpetual contemplation of an infinite glory.'

"My mind still clung to the image of my wife. A thought crossed my mind: I didn't even know if she were still alive. I knew only one thing — which I have learned well by now: Love goes very far beyond the physical person of the beloved. It finds its deepest meaning in his spiritual being, his inner self.

"Whether or not he is actually present, whether or not he is still alive at all, ceases somehow to be of importance.

"I did not know whether my wife was alive, and I had no means of finding out; but at that moment it ceased to matter. There was no need for me to know; nothing could touch the strength of my love, my thoughts, and the image of my beloved."

At first, Viktor – and fifteen hundred others sent to Auschwitz with him – were kept in a shed meant to hold only a fraction of that many people. The ground was bare, and the prisoners were forced to squat for days while they subsisted on only a small piece of bread. From here, the prisoners were directed into two lines – one to the gas chamber and the other to survival and labor.

Frankl's mother was executed in the gas chambers and he barely escaped that same fate. He was ordered to get into the left line, but defied the order and stepped into the other group. Only later did he discover the left line led to certain death.

The key to his survival in the camps, he would later say, was his ability get above his circumstances and externalize the situation.

> "I repeatedly tried to distance myself from the misery that surrounded me," he said. "I remember marching one morning from the camp to the work site, hardly able to bear the hunger, the cold, and pain of my frozen and festering feet, so swollen.
>
> "My situation seemed bleak, even hopeless. Then I imagined that I stood at a lectern in a large, beautiful, warm and bright hall. I was about to give a lecture to an interested audience on

"Psychotherapeutic Experiences in a Concentration Camp" (a title he later used). In the imaginary lecture I reported the things I am was living through. Believe me, at that moment I could not dare to hope that some day it was to be my good fortune to actually give such a lecture."

In April of 1945, Frankl was liberated. That summer he put his experience in writing. He dictated the first draft of the manuscript that was to become "Man's Search for Meaning" in nine days.

By 1946, he was fully back into his professional world, running the Vienna Polyclinic of Neurology. He began teaching at the University of Vienna, where he would remain as a professor until 1990. He remarried in 1947 and had two daughters with his wife Eleanor.

By the mid 1950s Frankl was being invited to speak at universities around the world. In 1955, the University of Vienna made him a full professor. By 1961, he was serving as a visiting professor at Harvard and his ideas were being cemented in the minds of those studying psychotherapy in the United States. His academic career continued to grow, as he lectured at over 200 universities and was awarded an astonishing 29 honorary degrees.

The Lost Interview

(Dr. Frankl agreed to sit down for an interview with me in May of 1985. The videotape of that interview has been lost through the years and many moves. Fortunately, this transcript remains.)

Bill Halamandaris:

Dr. Frankl, this is a great pleasure for me. I have been looking forward to meeting you and talking with you for some time.

One of the things that I find interesting is that when I talk to people about your work, the perception many of them of them have is that your work was generated by the experience of the concentration camp; that it was a result of that experience.

My understanding is that this is not the case and that you had your theories pretty well developed and a manuscript in hand when you were sent to the concentration camp. Is that correct?

Viktor Frankl:

I had hidden the manuscript of the first version of a book that in English at the end of the fifties was published under the title: *The Doctor and The Soul – from Psychotherapy to Logotherapy.* The manuscript was hidden in my overcoat when I arrived at the Auschwitz concentration camp. Of course, it was immediately destroyed, thrown away and so forth.

I reconstructed the manuscript there, writing on scraps of paper. The experiences I had to go through in the concentration camps then served as a validation of my theories. The theories had been built up already but it was an exemplification and a validation.

Through the effect that, in truth, it is the orientation toward a meaning to fulfill in the future, in the after liberation, that people, more than any other factor in even circumstances, those people have the most, the greatest chance to survive even this, let me say, abyss experience. Those people, I repeat, who had a vision of a future in freedom where they could either devote themselves again to a task, a life task as it were, to complete and or to be reunited with their loved ones.

And this is a manifestation, to speak in a broader context, a manifestation of what I have come to call the self-transcendent quality of a human being.

Primarily, basically, any human being is not – and I say this in contradiction to the current psychological theories – a human being is never primarily or basically concerned with himself or herself, or anything within himself or herself; but rather reaching out into the world, out of themselves, into the world toward a meaning to fulfill or another human being to love.

Bill Halamandaris:

So would you then be critical then of what has been called the "me" generation in this country where everything is focused on how I look, what I do, and how I dress. The result seems to be a great deal of emptiness and a great deal of dissatisfaction. Is that the kind of manifestation you are describing?

Viktor Frankl:

It is absolutely to the point what you have just said. In as much as people again and again approach me with the blame that – approach me with the reproach that I neglect the concept of self-actualization. Man should actualize himself, should actualize all the potentials he has within himself.

It would be OK, but it never can be made into an aim, into a target of our intentions, made into the purpose of life. Because anything – such as happiness, success, and particularly the encompassing, more encompassing concept of self-actualization – can only result as an unintended side effect of our dedication to something out into the world rather than within myself.

Namely, to meaning fulfillment. Once we have fulfilled the meaning out there in the world, not caring for ourselves' actualization we have reason to experience happiness.

Second, in the long run we may wind up with success by not caring neither for happiness nor success and least of all for self-actualization.

I wonder if it is of interest in this context to mention that only recently I came to know that Harvard University is issuing all of the diaries of the late great psychologist of your country, Abraham Maslow, who is in a way the originator of the concept of self-actualization.

And, within those diaries, he explicitly states, "Viktor Frankl has convinced me that self-actualization can not be a goal per se in itself, but can only be reached on a detour around the world by dedicating oneself, to selfless goals – not caring for self-actualization, but caring for things to do or people to encounter – and the side effects are happiness and success."

Bill Halamandaris

How does a person accomplish that goal? If a young person comes to you and is uncertain how to proceed, how should they begin this process? How do they start?

Viktor Frankl

You see, Goethe, the great German poet, centuries ago stated, "How can a man have knowledge of himself? Never by contemplation, but solely through action."

Do what is your duty or your responsibility. But what is your responsibility? The demands of the hour, of the moment.

So by listening carefully to what a situation is demand of you, by listening carefully to what your conscience – which I regard to be the prompter, built in a human being on the way, on the avenue to meaning fulfillment, by listening carefully – and then by going on to obey your conscience you will find out what is the meaning of the situation.

When people, say logotherapist, the followers of my psychotherapeutic theories, speak or refer to meaning, they don't have in mind the meaning of life, the meaning of mankind, the meaning of the world, of the universe, or anything like this.

But down to earth, the meaning of a given situation confronting you, the meaning of a concrete situation that pertains, that is a challenge to a concrete person.

Each situation in a way in life is unrepeatable and each person is ultimately someone who is irreplaceable.

From this two-fold uniqueness comes, emerges the mandatory, obligatory, demand upon someone. But, you see this comes very close, this speaking not of the meaning in life in logotherapy, but of a meaning in life in a given situation, addressed a call for fulfillment of this very meaning addressed to a given person.

This is emphasized in logotherapy and from this two-fold uniqueness emerges our sense of responsibility. Because, if you allow me to quote someone who was living about 2,000 years ago, no less than 2000 years ago, and is regarded as the founder of one of the first two Talmud schools.

I am referring to Hillel, a name that is virtually unknown among Gentiles at least in Austria, but well known in this country due to the so-called Hillel foundations on various campuses.

Any way, Hillel had a motto, and you may find it in the Holy Scriptures, to the effect: "If I do not do it, who will do it? If I do not do it now, when shall I do it? But, if I do it only for my own sake, what am I?"

First, if I do not don't do it who else will do it? This refers to the uniqueness of this person.

If I don't do it right now when shall I do it? This refers to the uniqueness of each passing transitory moment that gives you a chance, the uniqueness of the situation waiting, demanding you fulfill the meaning potentially at that moment.

And finally, if I do it only for my own sake, say in the lines of psychoanalytic fields is for the sake of getting tranquility attention less state of an equilibrium without being plagued and bombarded by driving instincts of the demands of this societal surroundings to do something or repress something and so forth.

Or, along the lines of Alderian psychology using literal quotations when I speak of those matters, that the aim of life is, the goal of life is really, ultimately nothing but trying to overcome the inborn inferiority feelings of each young individual of each child and to overcome it by compensating this feeling through a superiority, striving for superiority or will to power.

I myself would not be willing or prepared to live for the sake of getting rid of the inner tension aroused by drives and instincts. Nor would it be satisfying to me, be a legitimate goal in my life just to overcome feelings of inferiority.

I wouldn't give a damn for them in themselves, nor for overcoming them for the sake of building up a way to power. What I seek is something that nothing to do with what is going on within myself, but in the world.

The world is waiting for you, waiting the day that you do something in it; that you change the situation for better, or that I do it.

But not that we care for nothing but introspectively looking into ourselves in order to find quietness and tranquility and compensation of this or that feeling and so forth.

And this is what is referred to by the great wise man of two millennia ago, Hillel, who said finally, "but if I do it only for myself what am I?"

No real human being I would venture to answer his question. No human being, which as such, who as such, is self-transcendent.

 That is to say caring for something out in the world or someone out in the world rather than being concerned within himself or herself or anything within him or herself.

Bill Halamandaris:

Is that what you mean when you write your theory is different in that most people call psychiatrists "shrinks" and when you –

Viktor Frankl:

Psychiatrists, what?

Bill Halamandaris:

"Shrinks."

Viktor Frankl:

Yes, "head shrinkers."

Bill Halamandaris:

And you say logotherapy is "stretch" --

Viktor Frankl:

I have not said this. It was said in a review of a book of mine, said in terms of summing up the real essence, the nucleus, the core of my teachings.

But in a way, of course, because we try not to impose any values, not to impose any weight on shoulders, not to impose a meaning, a pre-given meaning, as it were, to anyone.

This is the job which has to be done and can be done justifiably by the priest, by the pastor, by the rabbi. But we are, personally I am and M.D. in addition to the Ph.D., but I scarcely mention the second degree because as I know my Viennese colleagues, nobody would say 'Oh, that guy, Dr Frankl, is a two-fold doctor.' No, they would say 'he is just half a physician.

Any way, this is exactly what I, what you have said before. This is correct. It is correct.

Bill Halamandaris:

You have written that essentially life challenges man, and that from that it follows that the essence of your philosophy is meeting that task.

The task, as you visualize it, is individual to each man and each purpose. Each of us must identify our task and find our own meaning in life. Is that correct?

Viktor Frankl:

Yes, but it doesn't make too much sense to ask respective questions, pertinent questions, because if you not only correctly and rightly understand what I wish to convey to my students and readers, you see, each situation implies a question addressed to you, to each of us, changing from man to man from moment to moment.

And, therefore, no general answers, universally valued answers can be given – by belief systems, of course – but not by a psychiatrist or psychologist.

More than that, no only universally valued questions can be given. But actually, ultimately, you have to reverse the whole situation, reverse the tables or something like that, because ultimately then what is at stake is that man understand himself or herself as the one who is asked a question, who has not the right, who is not justified in asking questions, but is the one who has to answer, to answer the questions that each situation poses for him, that each situation implies.

And that way we make a Copernican turn. Once we understand that it is we who have to respond rather than question – question the meaning of life rather than respond to life – we arrive at a deepened concept of responsibility. We have to answer the questions that life is asking us and we can only answer those questions, we can only respond to them, by being and feeling responsible for our actions and the action are the answers.

Bill Halamandaris:

Have your theories been modified over time? Have you found any revisions necessary?

Viktor Frankl:

First of all, I myself have been surprised and astonished to see time and again that the real substance of my theories has been developed already in my first publications.

Not only in 1924 when Sigmund Freud published a paper I had written as a sixteen-year-old boy, but also latter in the respective publications, articles, professional magazines and journals, many of which have been reprinted in my last book, published in Germany. And I'm surprised to see that actually the main tenants of logotherapy, tenable until today, have been laid down at that time.

But second, I could contribute a large store of case material exemplifying the validity of my theories. And even more important, my former students today doctors, professors, and so forth have contributed empirical evidence that show the validity also on strictly scientific methodologies.

Even those people who originally could have been my adversaries fighting my principles have turned to accept them ever more. But mainly, primarily, not the theories but the practices, the techniques, the methodology in treatment.

And so, there is an ever more growing sense and spirit of cooperation. Those who are closed-minded rather than open-minded and represent as it were closed systems as their own systems and don't allow to mingle with them or their representatives, they are as persons immature.

If you are a mature person you are a self-transcendent person and look out for transcending you own system and for cooperation.

We are open in a two-fold sense or have to be open in a two-fold sense, as I see it personally, in a two-fold direction I could say as well. That is to be open to what neighboring systems and to be open to the evolution of own systems.

And this is important to a guy like me who is in his 83 year of age and has to look out, to be prepared, to have prepare his legacy to be handed over, passed on to his former students or his representatives as it were.

Bill Halamandaris:

You mentioned that your first papers were written when you were 16 years old.

You have me wondering where this came from? Do you remember?

Viktor Frankl:

This is, you see, it deals with the origin of mimic expressions of affirmation and ligation. It is a very periphery problem, an issue all-together.

But as a high school student I was in correspondence with Sigmund Freud through out several years. And once I responded to a letter of his, he answered within 48 hours.

Once I enclosed without thinking any further, I enclosed a small manuscript and his reaction was, "Mr. Frankl, the manuscript you enclosed I forwarded to the *International Journal of Psychoanalysis*.

There it was published two years later. This was in 1924 and then, in that same year; I entered the Alderian Society, which is referred to today more often than not as the Second Viennese School of Psychotherapy over against Freud's first school.

One year after publishing in the *International Journal of Psychoanalysis,* Adler published a paper of mine in the *International Journal of Individual Psychology.*

A year later, in 1926, I already was publishing my own journal along, mainly the lines of Alderian theories, but also along my own lines as it were. And one year later, in 1927, I was because I was too little orthodox, excluded the house of the Alderian Society.

From then on, I went my own way. But you see, recently a documentary movie has been filmed by Austrian television. They filmed in Vienna, Austria and they filmed me standing at the entrance door of the house where I was born.

The cameraman turned up and focused on the street number, Jenning Street –

Jenning was a count and politician in Austria – number 6. And while they did so, it came to mind you should turn around with the camera to the opposite house on the same street.

Right there, 6, 8 and so forth and to the left there are 7, 9, and so fourth. I asked them to focus on number 7 and they asked why. Because here through the years Alfred Alder was living and practicing.

And it's interesting because it serves as a symbol. I was Alderian for 2 or 3 years, so our ideas are very close to one another and still opposite to one another. Like the houses, very close, just across the street, but very opposite to one another.

Bill Halamandaris:

That's a wonderful analogy…You have obviously known and worked with some great men – Adler, Freud, and all of these people. I am wondering who are the people who stand out in your mind as being the most significant or having the greatest influence on your life?

Viktor Frankl:

The first was a gentleman whom I noticed walking through the park – a park that today in Vienna is called, Sigmund Freud Park – an old gentleman with a worn out hat and worn out overcoat with a black walking stick beating the ground nervously with a silver handle and moving his jaws as if he was soliloquizing – soliloquy or whatever you call it.

And it suddenly came to me this guy looks like Sigmund Freud. That man cannot be Sigmund Freud, of course, but to be sure, let's follow him.

If he walks from the university close to the site, close to the university bearing street and then makes the right turn to Bercasa – Bercasa 19 is a famous address – it must be Sigmund Freud.

So, I followed him and when he made the turn I stopped him on the street. There was little traffic at the time. I asked him do I have the honor to speak with Professor Freud?

"Yes, that's me," he said.

I said, "My name is Viktor Frankl."

He said, "Wait a minute. Jenning Street, number 6, apartment number 25, second district of Vienna. Is that correct?"

"Absolutely, it is."

Then we talked for a while. We talked about a book someone in France had written about the death instinct. He said he wanted me to write a review.

Any way, we talked together and he was one of the men to your question. He was one of the men who served to me as what I regard to be equally important –

particularly for young people – namely, not only having a meaning in life but also having examples and models to emulate, to follow. One of them for me was Sigmund Freud.

Because I have lived at the same time when he was ridiculed, when people were laughing at him and dismissing his theories. And the pretext is just, I remember literally a statement in a famous magazine, intellectual magazine of Austria in the '30s, saying, "psychoanalysis is nothing but pornography under the camouflage of science."

But Freud did not let himself be discouraged by being unsuccessful among, at least among purely scientifically oriented people. He went his way without being discouraged by lack of success.

I too was ridiculed. May I mention, that in your country the first review of one of my first books – *Man's Search for Meaning* – was published in *The American Journal of Psychotherapy* along with a group of books that were being reviewed at that time – other books about concentration camps and bordering problems.

You know what the only remarkable thing was that the reviewer mentioned in his review? That Frankl in his book mentions an episode where from one can draw the conclusion that what took place in the individual prisoners of concentration camps was a personal regression. That was he whole review.

Now, Freud has destroyed a taboo: The taboo that is of sex. There were precedent people, of course, heralding, but any way he is credited with having destroyed a taboo. I have also destroyed a taboo. Do you know what taboo it was?

There was a novel that a couple of years ago was published in your country. *Natalie, Natalie* is the title of the thing. And in this novel there occurs a sentence: "Like at the times of Sigmund Freud, when there was a taboo concerning sex, now days we are confronted with another taboo. It is the taboo to do or speak of life as if it had any meaning at all."

This nihilism is what I try to fight. What I had fought already in my young years and had tried to over come by building up thoughts and later systematizing them by way of a theory – a theory that contradicts the wide spread feeling of meaninglessness today, and tries to convince people, to show people that life does have a meaning, a meaning, to be sure, that has to be discovered by each single individual again and again, day by day.

But there is a meaning waiting for each of us to be fulfilled in each situation, even the worst situations, in the most miserable situations, tragic situations confronting an individual with death, with pain, with suffering and with guilt.

And that is what I try to use upon myself, as well, because there is a theory to the effect that each person who has built up a psychotherapeutic system in this very system does nothing but offer, show up his own case history as it were.

It is well know that Freud was fighting and dealing with his own phobia of railway rides and that Adler was suffering from inferiority feelings.

So I was suffering from the feeling that apparently after all I had learned left me dissatisfied and life is just meaningless. And I tried and succeeded in overcoming this and building up a system.

Why should this system not be offered and be left to other people who have to try to overcome their feelings of meaninglessness?

Bill Halamandaris:

When you look at what is happening around us and you look at what has happened since you developed this theory, are you optimistic about the future? Do you think we are making progress?

Viktor Frankl:

I am rather skeptical about the future, but I know one thing, I know how much justification is implied in a statement by a famous German poet nearly two hundred years ago to the effect that wherever there is a disease, exactly there in that area also is that herb, a plant is growing which may well serve as the antidote.

For instance, where there are, where there is water, much water, people start suffering from rheumatism; there also you will find growing those trees from which you may produce aspirin, salicylic acid.

And so I think that when technology was growing, when people ever more were sitting through eight hours at the office at one time, mankind started coming up with sports, more and more sports, as compensation, as a self-help, and in this way you may watch and observe whatever is going down. Mankind finds a remedy for all that. But how long this will be possible is a question in itself.

You see, Sigmund Freud when he developed his system came up with the statement that if you expose a group of individuals, different personalities to one and the same situation of starvation, you will soon notice that they become uniform – uniformly just being concentrated on their drive to get food.

But in the concentration camps – Freud was spared to get to know a concentration camp – in the concentration camps we saw something different.

People became evermore different when confronted with such tragic situations like a concentration camp and believing they are ever more different. There, people unmasked themselves – both the swine and the saint.

Bill Halamandaris:

Dr. Frankl, you say your experiences were contrary to Dr. Freud's prediction that people will react identically in restricted circumstances – particularly starvation and poverty. Would you elaborate on that?

Viktor Frankl:

When I say people were unmasking themselves, both the swine and the saint, you should think about Maximillion Colbert who offered his life for someone else.

And you may have been taught that, OK, these are exceptions to the rule. You are right. Decent people, really decent people, really human people, we may say as well, form a minority.

But isn't this minority exactly what constitutes a challenge to ourselves? The challenge to follow them, to join them.

And this is what we have to feel the responsibility to 'do something'. Even if at the risk that we will flounder, we will go astray, this in fact the danger today.

In two ways, first in as much as we now, our generation now knows, the generation I mean after Auschwitz, after Dachau, after Mauthausen we know what man is capable of.

Man is the individual who has invented the gas chambers to be sure, but he is also the individual who has entered these very gas chambers, head held high and with dignity.

And in addition, we are not only living in a time when we have got to know what man is capable of, but also at the time when we know what is at stake. This is not only the time after Auschwitz, but at the same time it is the time after Hiroshima and so forth.

So we have to be alert, we have to do our best, whatever we can each of us, we have to meet our being responsible. An education should be not only education toward knowledge but also an education toward refining young people's conscience, conscience as I put it before is the prompter who gives us a vision of what can be done and what should be done.

Bill Halamandaris:

When you think of that time and the lives that were lost and the potential that was wasted and the terrible things that you saw, some that were done to you, do you have any bitterness?

It is remarkable to me that could come through an experience that dehumanizing and come out with a philosophy that is so human. Where does that come from?

Viktor Frankl:

You see people again and again ask me the question after the four concentration

Camps, being liberated by Turks in Bavaria, why did you return to Vienna?

Have they done too little bad things to you and your family? Your mother has died in the gas chamber of Auschwitz. Your father died at Treblinka. Your brother has died in the coal mine in Auschwitz. Your first wife died in Bergen Belsen. Is it too little they have done to you?

And I say, what have they done to me?

In Vienna there is an old baroness, was an old baroness at the time, who rescued the life of a cousin of mine by hiding her throughout the years in her domicile.

And in addition, there was a socialist lawyer in Vienna who had scarcely any intimate relationship with me, but we saw each other for a couple of years because I was living close to his office. He brought me food each time he saw me. At his life's danger. The same as the Catholic baroness.

Now why shouldn't I return to a country or a city that has brought forth such personalities?

There is no collective guilt. This is a lie. There is no collective guilt, but only personal guilt.

You can hold responsible someone only for what he has done personally, or has omitted to do personally. But you cannot condemn him for something that a population has done and least of all can you condemn or hold responsible people for what their ancestors, their parents, their grandparents have done or have omitted to do. That is absolute nonsense.

And generalizing small statements the toll that this has been taken has been experienced by Jews in Europe through out the Hitler regime.

So is this lesson too little a lesson?

And everywhere this can happen. In principle, everywhere anti-Semitism, nationalism, chauvinism, concentration camps, holocausts for that mater, are not a monopoly of the German population including or not including the Austrian one.

There is no monopoly in each territory; in each country this can happen again and again.

I wonder if you are familiar with the experiment where it was shown that people in principle are capable of, exposed to an authoritarian dictate, to apply electroshocks and life danger, and every thing like that.

So no left, the right hand should not pride itself that it has not been afflicted the other hand because it's the whole organization that has become ill. It is mankind as a whole that is threatened by going such ways in each country, on each continent, and each authoritarian and totalitarian regime.

And this is what I was indicating before. But skeptical not to say even pessimistic as we may be, we must not be nihilistic.

We must retain the sense of responsibility, being responsible in front of a task in wait for each of us, for each nation, and for each person.

Bill Halamandaris:

A couple more questions as we wrap this up. How would you like to be remembered? How would you like people to think of you?

Viktor Frankl:

Many years ago in the '60s or so, there was sitting around my desk at my hospital a group of three sabbatical professors from you country who had spent their sabbatical year to do research in the field of logotherapy and some students.

As usual about nine or ten in the morning I came to my office and greeted them.

But his time I had an envelope in hand already sealed. And with self-irony I asked them, "Guess what is here?"

I told them it was a request from the editor of Who's Who in America. They had written me up in several columns to describing my life or my life's work.

They asked me to sum it up in one sentence. One hundred people had been selected of the many thousands that were written there and I was one of them mentioned and I was asked in one sentence to epitomize my life and so forth.

"Guess what I wrote them," I said.

And one of the students stood up and said, "Professor, let me try. You have told them that you have seen the meaning of your life in helping others to see in their lives a meaning." It was exactly word-by-word what I had written and deposited in that letter already.

I mentioned before that one of the examples to follow, one of my spirited models not to say mentors was Sigmund Freud. Remember, I said that he did not let himself be discouraged by being unsuccessful.

Now there was another one. It was Martin Heidegger, the founder of the existentialism by way of over simplification.

And I was lucky enough to meet him personally in West Germany, and then he repaid me and came to my home in Vienna. And we had hours of long discussions – about the misunderstandings in your country prevailing in the field of existentialist philosophy, among other things by the way.

When I visited him, he showed me his study, library, with all the shelves and books and with his prepared manuscripts lying among them. *Being and Time*, side by side, his main – his fundamental work that was published I believe in 1927.

It was a huge success. Made him immediately world wide known. But on the title you found Part I; and there it lay in the '60s in his study the manuscript for Part II.

And until his death he did not allow it to be published because he no longer was in absolute agreement with what he had written down in 1927.

His philosophical conscience did not allow something to be published that was not, no longer behind which no longer stood. He obeyed his conscience in this respect. So he did not allow his fame and his success to entice him to publish something hurriedly that was no longer felt right.

And to see this, not being enticed by popularity to do something against one's conscience, in the same way that Freud did not let himself be discouraged by his not being successful – these are the models a young man in the field of science of philosophy or psychology, or psychiatry, for that matter, should follow. This impressed me.

You see, when I started by professional life – I evade career – it was not exactly what I was seeking in my life, making a career, I started with three wishes:

I wanted to become a psychiatrist. I became a psychiatrist.

I wanted to be a good psychiatrist. I hope I was not one of the worst psychiatrists.

And the third wish was I wanted to remain a human being. I'm still wrestling with this wish to fulfill.

***

The Last Lesson
May 1996

Shortly before he died, Dr. Frankl sent me the copy that follows for my review and comment. By this time, I knew he was more interested in sharing his perceptions than my critical evaluation. I don't know what, if any, use was ever made of the final document, if there even was one, or if this was just one more way to share his thinking with those of us he was "working on."

Facing the Transitoriness of Human Existence

How can we face, and cope with, our lives transitoriness; in other words, how is it possible to say yes to life in spite of death? Doesn't our mortality sweep out any meaning from our being? And how should we endure a life without any trace if meaning?

Our existential situation looks even worse in view of the fact that the transitoriness of human existence is a total and radical one: what is threatened and at last killed by death is not only life as a whole but each moment is passing by and dying away. Throughout our life span, at any time, everything says goodbye to us, adding, "won't see you later again."

But upon closer scrutiny it turns out that the only thing that really is transitory is the potential meaning offered by each moment – its meaning potential; the opportunity to actualize such a potentiality, to convert a possibility into a reality.

In fact, I wouldn't hesitate to formulate the very definition of meaning by stating that, in the final analysis, that which we perceive as meaning, is some sort of Gestalt; but the perception of meaning differs from the classical concept of Gestalt perception insofar as the later implies awareness of a "figure" on a "ground", whereas the perception of meaning boils down to becoming aware of a possibility against the background of reality, or to express it in plain words, to becoming aware of what can be done about a given situation. And the very challenge to so something about a situation is that which makes for what the founders of Gestalt psychology, Kurt Lewin and Max Wertheimer, called its "demand characteristic" or "demand quality."

Anyway, life thus seen as a chain of potentials to be actualized, possibilities to be realized, and meanings to be fulfilled makes us understand why Hebbel once came up with the statement, "Life is not anything but an opportunity to do something."

As to death, however, it now turns out to be no more than a mere terminal, the point at which our lifelong dying process around ourselves eventually winds up.

But we would also, as it were, do injustice to death by believing that it deprives and robs life of meaning; actually, it doesn't take the meaning away from, but rather gives meaning to life.

Just imagine what would happen if our life were not finite, if we were immortal: wouldn't we be justified in postponing everything?

Nothing would have to be done today for we could do it as well tomorrow, next week, next month, or next year – postponing it ad infinitum. Only under the threat and pressure of death does it make sense to do what we can and should, right now, that is, to make proper use of the moment's offer of a meaning to fulfill – be it a deed to do, a work to create, anything to enjoy, or a period of inescapable suffering to go through with courage and dignity.

If we are being in search of meaning, meaning – as we now can see – is in no way done away with by death; but the fact that death is in wait for us does make for enhancing our sense of responsibility, of being responsible beings.

At this point, allow me to intersperse a personal reminiscence: Forty-five years ago, I stood on the ramp of a railway station of a place called Auschwitz.

At that time, the probability that I would survive was 1 to 29 as can be statistically evidenced. Now you may understand that, if such an individual actually survives, he will ask himself day by day whether he has also been worthy of survival, that is to say, whether he has made proper use of each and every day, and he will have confess: only partially, if at all.

And psychiatrists, particularly in your country, have come up with the concept of survivor's guilt.

I don't thing that this concept is a legitimate one; I rather think what the majority of the survivors of concentration camps have been experiencing may be called "survivor responsibility."

Because what they feel is a deep sense of being responsible, of having carefully to listen to what the prompter called conscience is whispering in their ears regarding the question of how to make the best of each single opportunity that life may hold for and offer them.

And now you may understand how come that I arrived later on – so to speak, in the post-Auschwitz-period of my life – at the formulation of a maxim which reads as follows: "Live as if you were living for the second time – and as if you had acted the first time as wrongly as you are about to act now."

Once an individual really puts himself into this imagined situation, he will instantaneously become conscious of the full gravity of the responsibility that every man bears throughout every moment of his life: the responsibility for what he will make of the next hour, for how he will shape the next day.

By what I have said, some among you may well be reminded of the famous saying by Hillel, starting with the words: If I'm not doing it – who will do it? And if I don't do it right now – when shall I do it?

This means pointing to the preciousness of the unrepeatable moment, and to the irreversibility of human existence – that irreversibility which heuristically is bracketed by the maxim: "Live as if you were living the second time…" so that the temporality of life temporally seems to e suspended.

But now let us come back to what has been said regarding the possibilities that alone are affected by the transitoriness of human existence. What did I thereby want to convey to you?

As soon as we have used an opportunity and have actualized a meaning potential, we have done so once and for all. We have converted a possibility into a reality, and as such we have rescued it into the past.

For in the past, nothing is irrecoverably lost but everything is irrecoverably stored; we have safely delivered and deposited it in the past because nothing and nobody can ever deprive us or rob us of what we have treasured in the past.

What we have done cannot be undone! To be sure, all the more we should be aware of our responsibilities, our being responsible for what to do, whom to love, and how to suffer.

Usually, people tend to see only the stubble fields of transitoriness but overlook and forget the full granaries of the past into which they have brought in, and saved, the harvest of their lives.

Let us not forget that "having been" is still a mode of being – perhaps even the safest mode. And in the phrase "being past," the emphasis is to be placed on "being."

In fact, when Martin Heidegger came to Vienna and honored me by visiting my home, he discussed, among other things, also this matter.

To express his agreement with my view on the past, he autographed his picture as follows:

> Das Vergangene geht;
> Das Gewesene komt.

In English, the translation is:

> What has passed, has gone;
> What is past, will come.

In this context, let me emphasize that whatever we have rescued into the past, remains therein irrespective of whether anyone remembers it or not; just as something exists, and continues to exist, irrespective of whether we look at it or not, and even continues to exist regardless of our own existence.

For a change, let's now discuss the issue in a more "down to earth" style, with special emphasis placed on its clinical, practical aspects. Let me therefore quote from a tape-recorded conversation I one had in front of my medical students in the classroom of the neurological department I had to run, throughout a quarter of a century, in one of Vienna's general hospitals.

The patient was a girl who had show feelings of meaninglessness, more specifically, in view of transitoriness.

"Sooner or later life will be over," she said, "and nothing will be left – surely nothing."

I tried to bring her to recognize that the transitoriness of her existence does in no way detract from its potential meaningfulness. But I was not successful, and so I embarked on what is called a Socratic dialogue.

"Have you ever met a man," I asked her, "whose achievement and accomplishment you have a great respect?"

"If there is anyone who has lived a life full of meaning, it was our family doctor – how he cared for his patients, how he lived for them…"

"He died?" I inquired.

"Yes," she answered.

"But his life was exceedingly meaningful, wasn't it?" I asked her.

"Certainly," she replied.

"And this meaningfulness – was it done away with at the moment of his death?" I asked.

"In no way," was her answer. "Nothing can alter the fact that his life was meaningful."

But I continued challenging her: "And what if not a single patient ever remembers what he owes to your family doctor, say, due to lack of gratitude?"

"Oh, no. His life remains something meaningful," she said.

"What about people forgetting him just due to the lack of memory?" I asked.

"It remains –"

"Or what about the possibility, nay, the probability that sooner or later the last of his patients will have died himself – will the meaningfulness of your doctor's life be annulled or –"

"No. It will remain."

Thus I eventually succeeded in getting across to that girl at least a clue to the effect that meaning once fulfilled has been fulfilled once and forever, that is to say is no longer subjected to, and affected by, transitoriness but "rescued to the past", as I put it before. It is sheltered from transitoriness!

But what about a life of short duration, say the life that ends too early? Well, I think that we are not justified to draw conclusions from the duration of anyone's life to its meaningfulness.

Do we judge a biography by its length? Say, by he number of pages that a biographical book comprises?

Don't we rather judge it by the richness of the respective life? Don't we know examples of people who died young, and yet, their existence had incomparably more meaning than the existence of some long-lived dullard?

But in this context we have also to consider those counseling situations where in it might be indicated. But there is no such case whose story could be told so briefly as the often-quoted case of a colleague of mine, the story of an old practitioner who consulted me because his of his depression after his wife had died two years before.

Again using Socratic dialogue, I restricted me comment to asking him what would have happened if not his wife, but he himself had died first.

"How terrible this would have been for her – how much she would have suffered," was his answer.

Whereupon I reacted by asking another question: "Well, Doctor, this suffering has been spared her, but you have to pay for it – by surviving and mourning her."

At that moment, he began to see his own suffering in a new light. He could see a meaning in his suffering – the meaning of a sacrifice he owed to his wife.

He was still mourning her; but he no longer was desperate – because, as I used to coach it in an equation: $D = S - M$. Despair is suffering without meaning.

But it is not only partners who die and leave us alone. It is also children who become the victims of the transitoriness of human existence while their parents live on and thus have to survive them. It is unbelievable to what extent the parents are capable of coping with such a fate.

Let me share with you one such incident. I am going to quote from a booklet authored by the late bishop George Moser who said he met a woman with an unusual bracelet made of baby teeth mounted in gold.

The bishop commented on it saying, "That's a beautiful bracelet."

"Yes," the woman answered. "This tooth belonged to Miriam, this one to Esther, and this one Samuel, mentioning the names of her nine children by age. "Nine children, and all of them take to the gas chambers."

Shocked, the man asked, "How can you live with such a bracelet?"

Quietly, the woman replied. I am now in charge of an orphanage in Israel."

This is a unique example of a human being bearing witness to the "human potential" at its best, which is the capacity to turn a tragedy into a triumph.

Often people are in despair not, like in the preceding case, because of having to survive their children, but rather, just to the contrary, because there are no children of their own who would survive their parents.

However, what underlines this type of despair is the assumption that a life with no children is ultimately meaningless, and this is a fundamental mistake because either life has a meaning, then it retains this meaning whether it is long or short, whether or not it reproduces itself; or life has no meaning, in which case it remains to meaningless no matter how long it lasts or can go on reproducing itself.

If the life of a childless woman was really meaningless solely because she had no children, then humanity lives only for its children, and the whole meaning of existence is to be found in the next generation.

But this is only a postponement of the problem. For every generation then hands the problem on to the next generation unsolved. The only meaning in the life of one generation would consist in raising the next. But if something is meaningless, it does not acquire meaning by being immortalized.

To sum up, the assumption that procreation is the only meaning of life, contradicts and defeats itself; for if life is meaningless of itself, it can never be made meaningful merely by its perpetuation.

From all of which we see once again that life can never be an end in itself, and that its reproduction can never be its meaning; rather, it acquires meaning from other, non-biological frames of reference, from sources that necessarily lie beyond itself.

To be bestowed with meaning, life must transcend itself; but in "height" – in the sense of spirituality growing beyond oneself – or in "breadth" in the sense of social engagement.

As to spiritual growth, however, it was Elizabeth Kubler-Ross who once coined, for one of her books, a title that epitomizes the last and greatest chance any human being may be given: *"Death, the Final State of Growth."*

To take the chance certainly presupposes heroism. But heroism is something that, as I see it, can be expected, or demanded, solely of one person, and that is – oneself!

One should, therefore, always avoid to approach aging, suffering, or dying people – if I may say so – with a moralistically raised finger – instead of a finger pointing, namely, pointing to an example given by someone who shows us how to die – and, as you know, in the history of philosophy someone has defined philosophy as *knowing* how to die.

When Sigmund Freud once complained in a letter to Lou Salome how hard it was to come to terms, after more than 30 surgical operations, with his chronic illness, she – in her reply – pointed out that there is a need to set an example.

To be sure, during "the final stage" his doctor gave a shot that spared the patient absolutely unnecessary – and in this sense, meaningless – pain in ultimis. Preceding this stage, however, Freud had devoted himself in the completion of his writings, and refused taking painkillers.

Of course, work itself may be considered at least a mild painkiller, relieving suffering at least in some degree. One of the greatest brain surgeons of all times, Cushing, once said, as an old man, to his friend and colleague Dandy: "The only way to endure life is always to have a task to complete."

And I personally cannot remember having seen so many books lying on someone's desk as on that of the psychiatrist (and great schizophrenia researcher) Joseph Berze when he was more than 90 years of age. He kept himself busy by reading and reading until his death.

Not to mention the classical example of Goethe who, as an old man, had been working throughout no less than 7 years on his "Faust" drama's part II. Only 2 months after the completion of his opus magnum, he died.

Also, it is only two weeks since the great etiologist, Konrad Lorenz, a Nobel laureate, died in Vienna at the age of 85 – also a few months after the completion of his last great work.

But it is not only work what keeps one alive and helps on "endure life," as Cushing put it; also enriching oneself through experiences may be helpful.

Let me, in this context, quote from a letter I once received from a lady. She wrote, "I am 87 years of age; but to me, each day is a gift and we must be grateful! Look – I can watch from my window, the wonderful park. I can talk to the trees. I am deaf; but my innermost self talks to me.

"What is important is to say "yes" to everything! Why can't people understand this? I cannot walk; but I can think, and this is something for which I am most grateful."

Who would not be reminded of the famous saying of Blaise Pascal who once defined man as "a reed – but a reed that thinks."

Of course, all this not only points out how important it is to keep oneself busy – by transcending oneself toward "a task to complete" – but it also should serve as an admonition not to stop being dedicated to something outside oneself.

In no way does this mean overrating an individual's capacity to continue working; but on the other hand, we must not understate the individual's capacity to mobilize coping mechanisms in the sense of compensating some deficiencies, at least to some amount.

I well remember my rock-climbing guide who, while watching me during a common tour through a steep mountain wall, commented on my rock climbing style.

"Listen, Doctor, while I observe your climbing – please, don't become angry," he said – "but as I see, you possess virtually no strength any more; but the way in which you compensate this lack of rude strength, compensating it through refined rock climbing technique – I must confess: from you one can learn rock climbing."

I nearly exploded from self-esteem; after all, the man who had said this to me had been leading a group on a tour of the Himalayas. Anyway, encouraged by him I continued my rock climbing until five years ago.

I have presented my convictions in a more or less anecdotical manner but there is also an increasing body of empirical studies confirming and corroborating my assumptions.

Gary T. Reker of Trent University presented a paper at the Annual Meeting of the Gerontological Society of America in San Francisco in 1988 on "Sources of personal meaning among young, middle-aged and older adults."

Using the Personal Meaning Index (PMI) as developed by him, he found out that "sources of meaning that go beyond hedonistic or self-serving needs," optimally "contribute to a global sense of meaning in life, supporting Frankl's view that a deeper sense of meaning can only be discovered when an individual moves toward a self-transcendent state."
Using the Purpose in Life Test (PIL) as developed by James C. Crumbaugh and Leonard T. Maholick, and using supportive logotherapy in the treatment of terminally ill patients, Terry Zuehlke and John T. Watkins reported that "the patients experienced a significant increase in the inner sense of purpose and meaning in their lives ("The use of psychotherapy with dying patients,"

Journal of Clinical Psychology, 1975 and "Psychotherapy with terminally ill patients," Psychotherapy: Theory, Research, and practice, 1977).

From all this you may see that not only suffering but also dying holds and offers a meaning potential. But since even death may be bestowed with meaning, life turns out to be potentially meaningful under each and every condition; that is to say, the meaning of life is unconditional!

And this, too, could be evidenced in strictly empirical terms. I refer to the research done by Brown, Casciani, Crumbaugh, Dansart, Duriac, Kratochvil, Lukas, Lunceford, Mason, Meier, Murphy, Planova, Popielski, Richmond, Roberts, Ruch, Sallee, Smth, Yarnell, and Young.

These authors have evidenced by tests and statistics that in fact meaning is available to each and every person – regardless of sex or age, IQ or educational background, environment or character structure, and – last but not least – regardless of whether or not one is religious, and if one is, regardless of the denomination to which one may belong.

But, behold, this unconditional quality of meaning is paralleled by an equally unconditional value of each and every human being – that unconditional value which usually is called dignity. And why is dignity something unconditional?

Because it must not be confounded with mere usefulness in terms of functioning for the benefit of today's society – a society that is characterized by achievement orientation and consequently adores people who are successful and happy, and in particular adores the young.

Thereby, to be sure, the decisive difference between being valuable in the sense of dignity and being valuable in the sense of usefulness is blurred. However, if you are not cognizant of this difference but believe that an individual's value depends on present usefulness, you owe it only to personal inconsistency if you don't go ahead and plead for euthanasia in the strictest sense of Hitler's program, that is to say, "mercy" killing of all those who have lost their social usefulness, be it because of old age, incurable illness, mental deteriation, or whatever handicap they may suffer.

And I possess some experience with regard to euthanasia under the Nazi because, together with my colleague, the head of the Psychiatric University Hospital of Vienna, Professor Otto Potzl, I was involved in illegally but successfully sabotaging euthanasia. (I used false certification where in I diagnosed fever delirium or endogenous depression, and aphasia instead of schizophrenia.)

Anyway, usefulness may have left a person but dignity will stay with him or her. And those who still cannot but have contempt for old people should take heed not to fall pray to self-contempt once they have grown old themselves and then are immersed in the nagging feeling of being inferior.

But there is no need to pity old people. For what reason should we pity them? Because they have no longer any opportunities in store for them, any possibilities in the future?

They have more than that. Instead of possibilities in the future, they have their realities in their past; their deeds done, the loves loved, and last but not least, the sufferings they have gone through with courage and dignity. In a word, they have already brought in the harvest of their lives, and now may, as it has been said in the Book of Job, come to their graves "like a shock of corn cometh in its season."

✳✳✳

Printed in Great Britain
by Amazon